I0477720

Always for the sake of the Almighty One, Who is The Reality of All Mirrors of Gratitude!

And to that Perfect Mirror, the principle of praise and beauty ... Muhammad!

And to the Sultan of Saints and my heart's succor, Mevlana Shaykh Nazim ... You grabbed me from the desert of forms to the dessert of heavenly norms!

And to my Muhammadan Pole of Power and Grace, Mevlana Shaykh Hisham! In your presence, I'm with the Hashemite King.

And to my spiritual mothers, Hajjah Amina and Hajjah Naziha, your Amana and Nazaha engulf us in the purity of al-Zahra!

And to the Seal of Muhammadan Sainthood, the Greatest Master Ibn 'Arabi. You are the reviver of my inner religion and spirit!

And to my parents, Zohair and Sawsan, you are the roses of my heart and wings with which I fly.

And to my Fatima Zahra ... with you I'm complete; you are who I want to be!

Contents

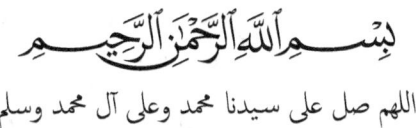

اللهم صل على سيدنا محمد وعلى آل محمد وسلم

Preface

By Divine Grace and a gaze from the Greatest Master, Muhyiddin Ibn al-'Arabi (QS), this entire book was conceived, compiled and published in one month.

Al-Shaykh al-Akbar (The Greatest Master) and *Khatm al-Walaya al-Muhammadiyya* (The Seal of Muhammadan Sainthood) is one of a few Muslim saints who often used diagrams to convey his rich and detailed *kashf* (unveiling) to the reader.

It is with the intention of bringing these precious renderings from the 'Beyond' to readers who are lovers of Sufism, Spirituality, Art and Ibn al-'Arabi that I am motivated to compile these nineteen diagrams, translate any terms therein to English and also include the Shaykh's guide to understanding the illustrations.

Before leaving you in the blessed hands of the Shaykh, I would like to offer a few remarks about this book.

First, aside from the last two diagrams, the other seventeen illustrations are all found in Ibn al-'Arabi's magnum opus *al-Futuhat al-Makkiyya* (The Meccan Openings). Eleven of these are found in a single chapter of this work, titled: "Regarding Knowing the Abode of a Secret and Three Secrets of the Tablet."

Second, although the Shaykh offers detailed information about some of the diagrams, his remarks about many of these eleven illustrations in chapter 371 are very terse. In order to maintain the integrity of his approach, I have chosen to leave those comments as they are found in the original text.

Third, in relation to the above point, I'm pleased to say that aside from this preface, the titles given to each diagram, which I have written with a supplication for a poetic license from the Shaykh himself, and a single disclaimer in the chapter "The Silent Cartography of Reality," all else in this book is Ibn 'Arabi's own words and drawings.

Therefore, you and I are one and the same. We are both stepping into the Shaykh's expansive grace and seeking his gaze, permission and love to allow us to receive, visually, what he wants his devoted readers to taste.

In many ways, these diagrams serve as a visual synthesis and summary of the Shaykh's entire thought. From this perspective, this book is a gift to artists who have an interest in Sufism and spirituality. They are those who intuitively know that art, like the Unseen, is to be tasted and contemplated, as opposed to categorized and rationalized.

This is also why I have chosen to place the Shaykh's written description of the diagrams after the illustrations themselves, a strategy which he often uses as well. This in order to allow the reader ample time to reflect upon the diagrams in their original Arabic and English renderings, prior to reading their explanations.

Lastly, the sudden urgency with which I have been motivated to finish this work has hindered me from redesigning the Arabic diagrams into a higher quality with a more readable terminology. Instead, I leave you with the hope of republishing this work in a second edition that will include these redesigned Arabic and also English diagrams.

With this, I take you and myself into this Akbarian ocean and ask God Almighty to bless us with receiving the infinite gaze, care and love of Ibn al-‘Arabi and all the saints who breathe, speak and write through the Reality of our Master Muhammad, countless prayers, blessings and salutations be upon Him!

ഇൗൽ

A Merciful Governance of All Things, Good and Bad

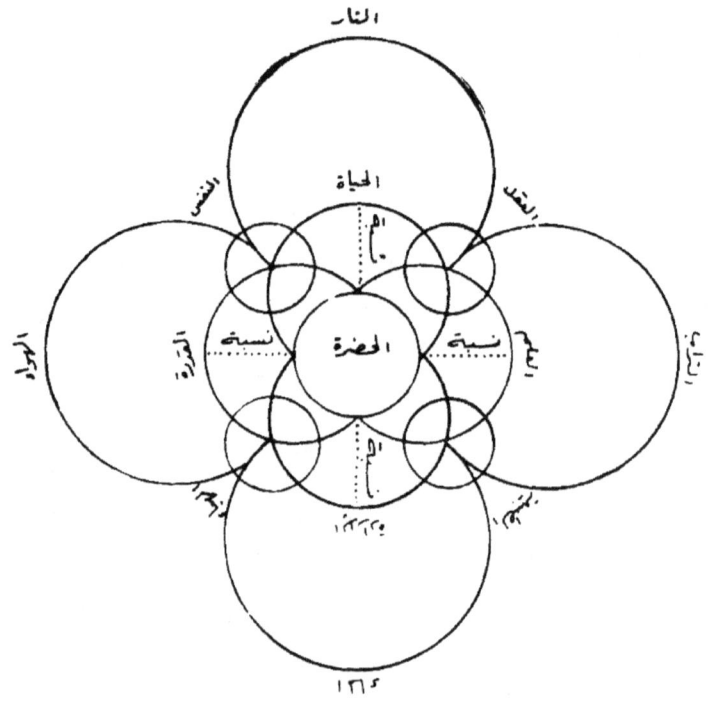

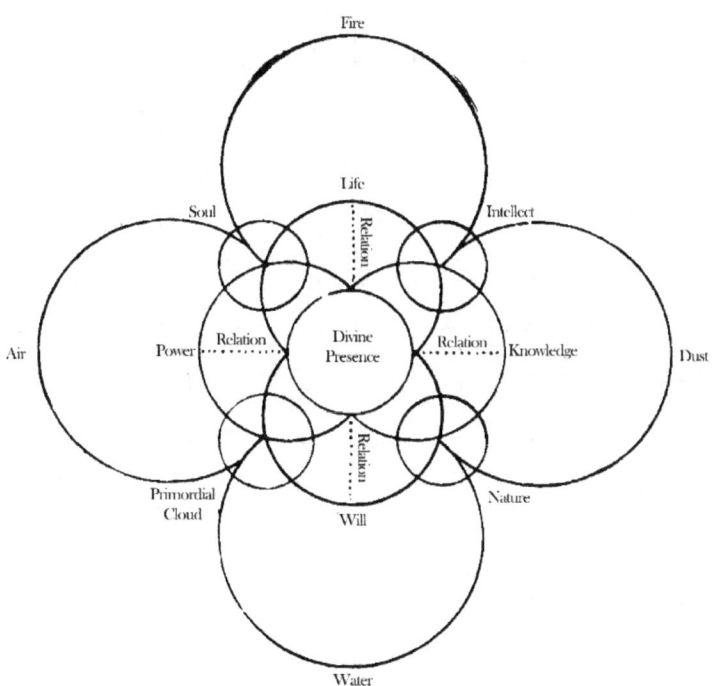

"Every line that emerges from the dot to the circumference is parallel to its neighbor and also arrives at another dot in the circumference. The dot in itself does not increase, despite the numerous lines that emerge from it to the circumference.

In this way, multiplicity has appeared from the Singular Essence, while He has not increased in His Essence.

Divine Will in this case is the line that emerges from the dot at the center of the circle to the circumference. This is the Divine Gaze which has brought all things that reside in the circumference into existence.

The circle itself contains universes, colors and what cannot be enumerated of types and persons. The origin of all of this is the first original dot."

- *The Meccan Openings*, Vol I, 393.

-

A Circle of Spiritual Life, from Prophets to Witnesses and Truth

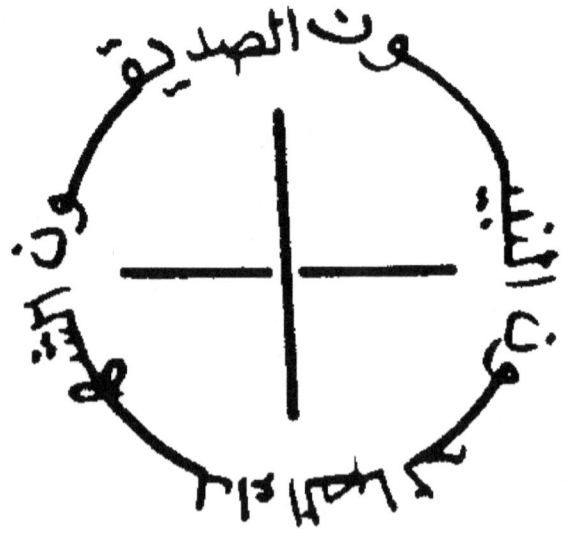

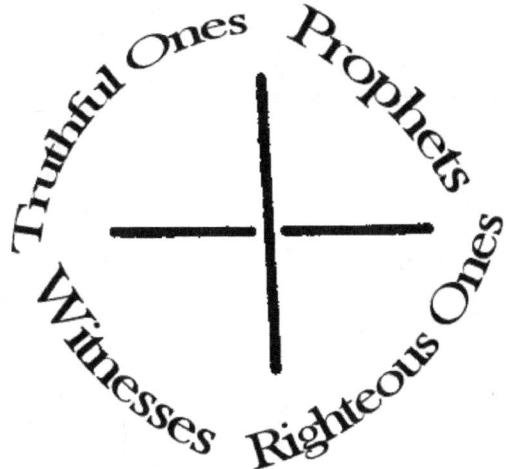

"I begin with Prophethood and end with Righteousness. If the circular shape is made such that the beginning is connected to the end, then the circle is correct.

This is because every prophet is a righteous person … Prophets are 'righteous' and fit for prophethood, that is why they are called righteous.

God then granted them proofs, whence they became witnesses.

He also informed them of the Unseen, whence they became truthful ones.

Thus, prophets are fit to occupy all these stations."

-   *The Meccan Openings,* Vol III, 40.

A Vision of Existence, in an Ancient Tome with Emptiness

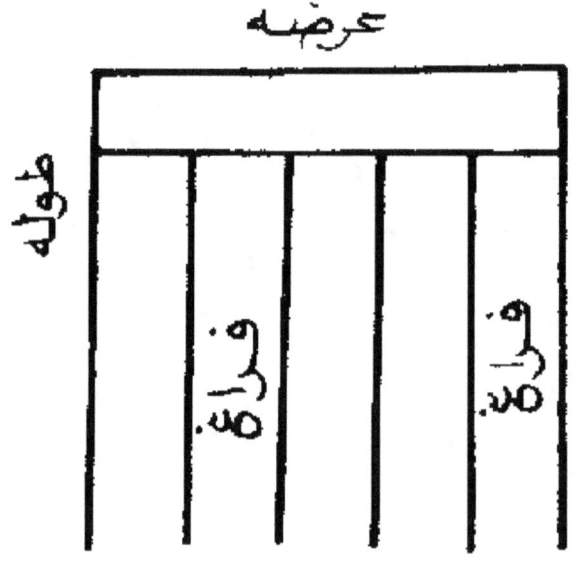

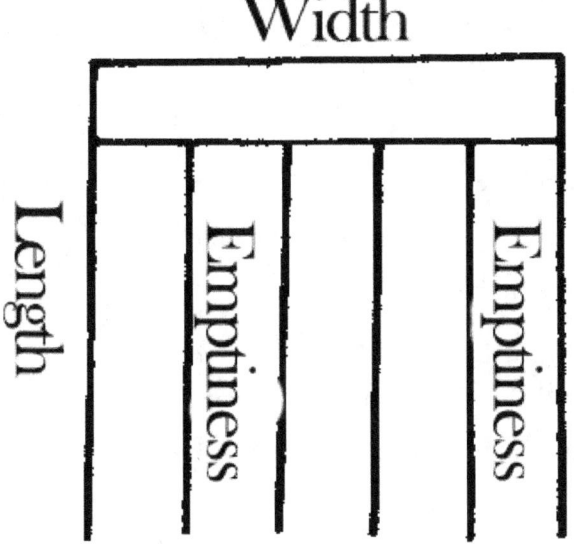

"The Twenty-Third way of affirming God's Oneness emerges from the Breath of the Most-Merciful. Since the entire world is the Words of God, each of their relationships to the Merciful Breath is singular. This would mean that there is no hierarchy in the world.

However, I have seen a wondrous vision that confirms a Oneness of hierarchy.

I was given a parchment whose width is over twenty arm's length, while its length I am unsure about. Its shape is as I have shown you here.

It is made from the skin of a sheep. While you are reading it, it appears white to you. When you look at it while not reading it, it appears green.

If you read it, it appears to be leather. If you do not read it, it appears to be made from fabric, either silk or linen."

- *The Meccan Openings*, Vol IV, 68.

From the Heights, Witness Gardens and Flame

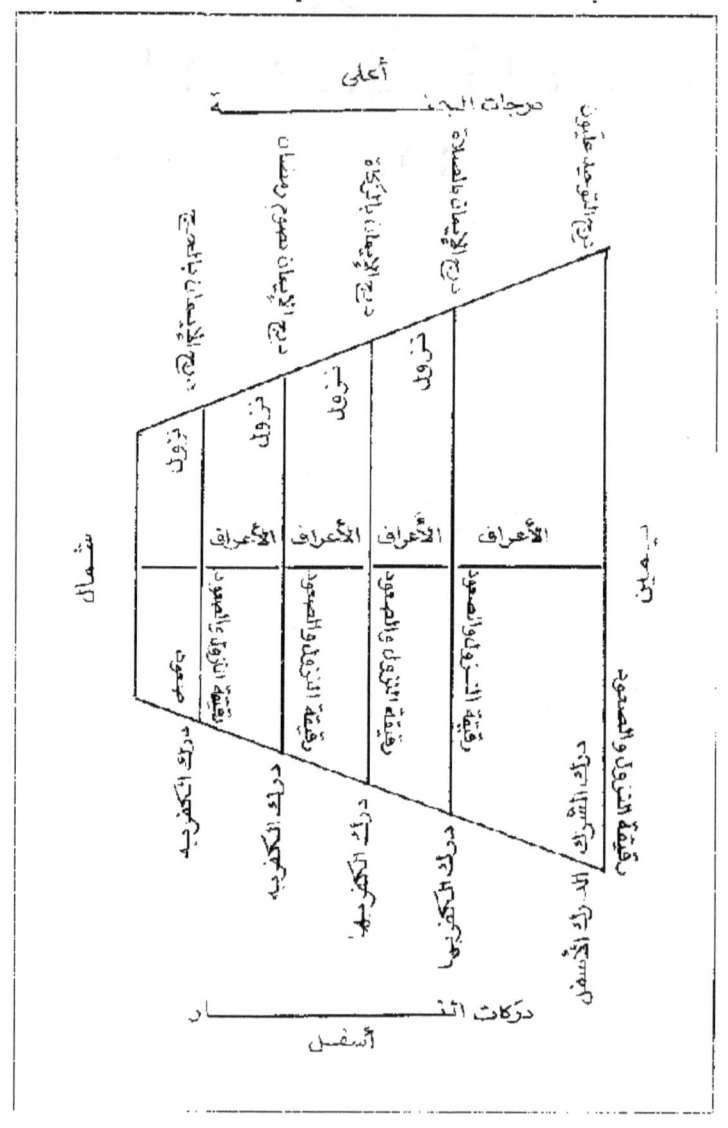

24

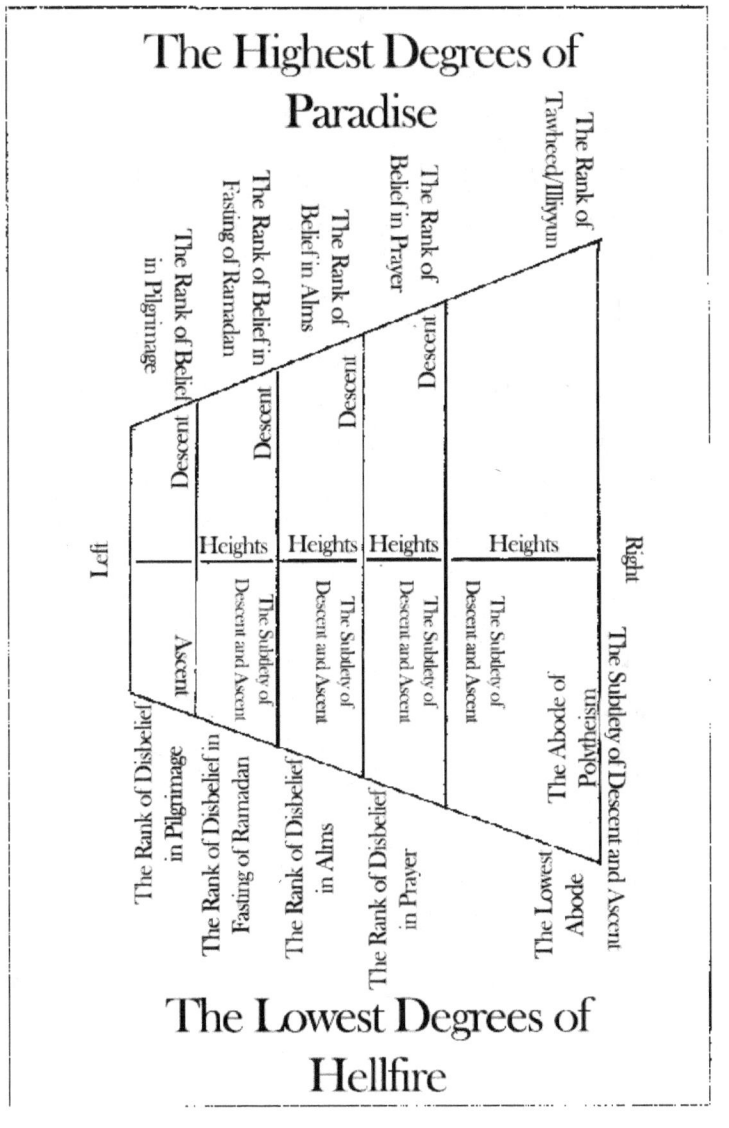

The Highest Degrees of Paradise

The Lowest Degrees of Hellfire

"We have detailed the affair of the Hereafter in parallel to the situation in this life, which can be seen in this shape symbolizing the pillars of Islam.

In this way, we should regard all the commands and prohibitions, whether it is an action or statement.

The image shows the ranks of Paradise and levels of Hellfire. The Heights is the wall whose inward is mercy and outward is punishment.

I have also written down the ascending and descending subtleties, so that you may imagine them in your mind, if understanding them abstractly is too distant from you."

- *The Meccan Openings*, Vol IV, 462.

An Intimate Circumference of Essence and Being

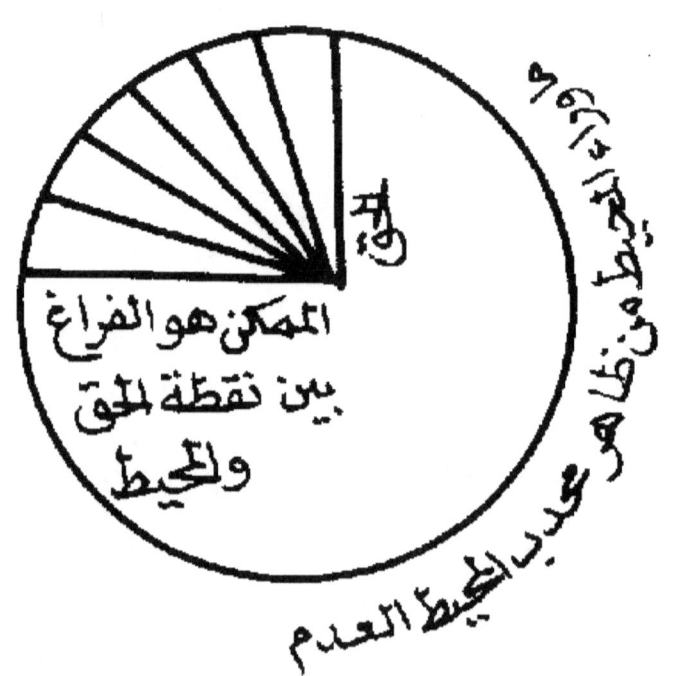

الممكن هو الفراغ
بين نقطة الحق
والمحيط

28

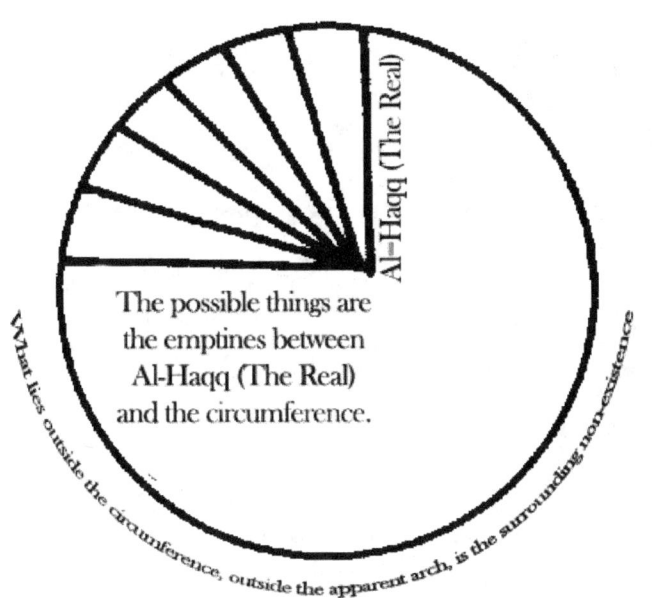

Al-Haqq (The Real)

The possible things are
the emptines between
Al-Haqq (The Real)
and the circumference.

What lies outside the circumference, outside the apparent arch, is the surrounding non-existence

"Let us pass beyond what people refer to as light or darkness, such as the lights attributed to stars, lamps or lighting, or even those darknesses recognized by the senses.

In actuality, these are merely metaphors of the realities of the Necessary Existent, impossible and possibly existent.

The Necessary Existent (God) has encompassed His own Reality and that of the sides (existence and non-existence). Indeed, this is the ocean of vast knowledge and great waves within which ships drown. It is an ocean without a shore, save its two sides.

It cannot even be imagined! If it must be put into form, then let it be a dot with a circumference. This dot is the Real, while the emptiness outside the circumference is non-existence and in-between them are the possible things."

- *The Meccan Openings*, Vol V, 406.

Everything Comes from the I of the Perfect One

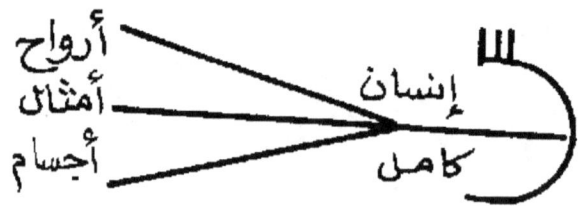

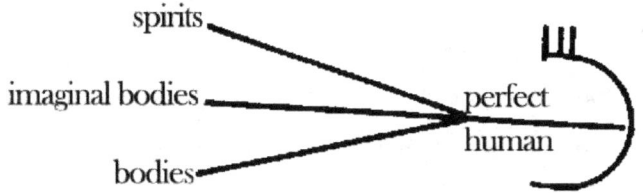

"There is none who brings into existence save God. He is the Creator of all things.

And the first key through which the Unseen has opened is the Perfect Man, who is the Shadow of God in everything other than God.

God made the Perfect Man appear from the Breath of the Most Merciful which is itself emerging from the Heart of the Qur'an, *Yaseen*.

This is why I have drawn the image of the Perfect Man in the Unseen in the likeness of a person's shadow.

Have you not seen how a person's shadow, when extended, merges with the other person standing in front of them?

Likewise, the human being is the shadow of God, he is hidden in appearance and appearing in the Unseen."

-    *The Meccan Openings*, Vol V, 412.

The Silent Cartography of Reality

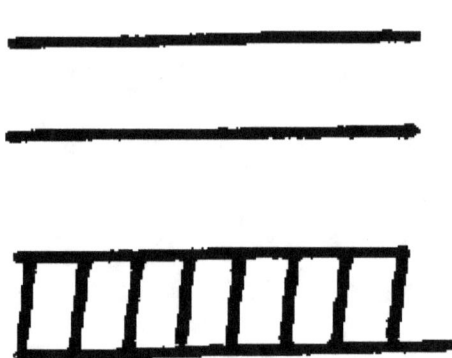

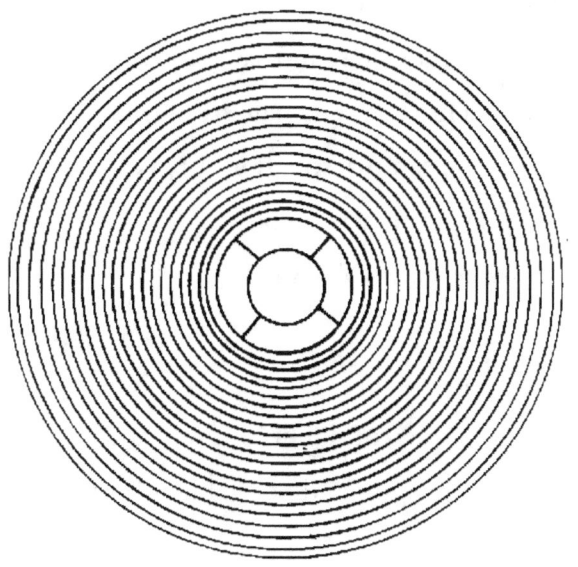

The preceding two diagrams are the only ones in *The Meccan Openings* that do not include any writings. He says about the first:

"The one who sees with two eyes takes the path of happiness which is not preceded by any misery. Indeed it is an easy pure road like a clean garment. Meanwhile, the other path, even though its end is happiness, includes difficulties and savage beasts. The two roads are adjacent. They emanate from one source and end at the same destination. I have envisioned and drawn them as such."

    -   *The Meccan Openings*, Vol VI, 181.

And about the second:

"This is an image of the world in its entirety and the ranking of its levels, in spirit and body, highness and lowliness.

The levels are: the 'Primordial Cloud', Throne, the outermost orbit, the orbit of stations, the abode of resurrection, hellfire, the presence of Divine Names, the paradisiacal musk and the entire created world."

    -   *The Meccan Openings*, Vol VI, 194-214.

The Art of Ibn al-'Arabi

What the Angels Lost
in Love See

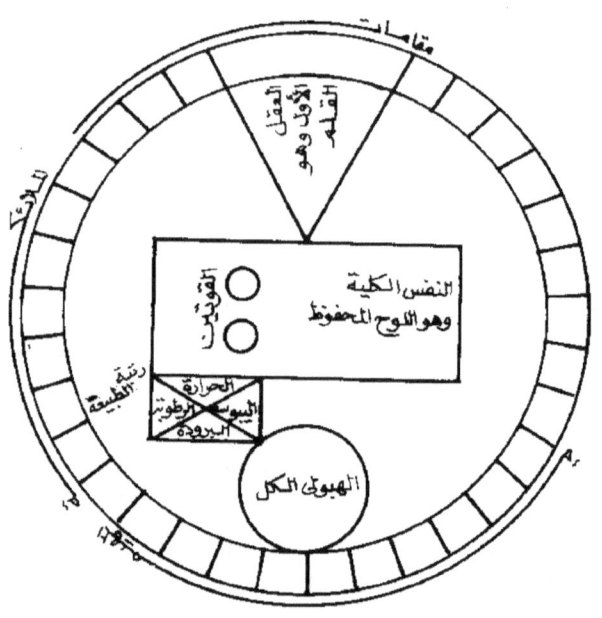

40

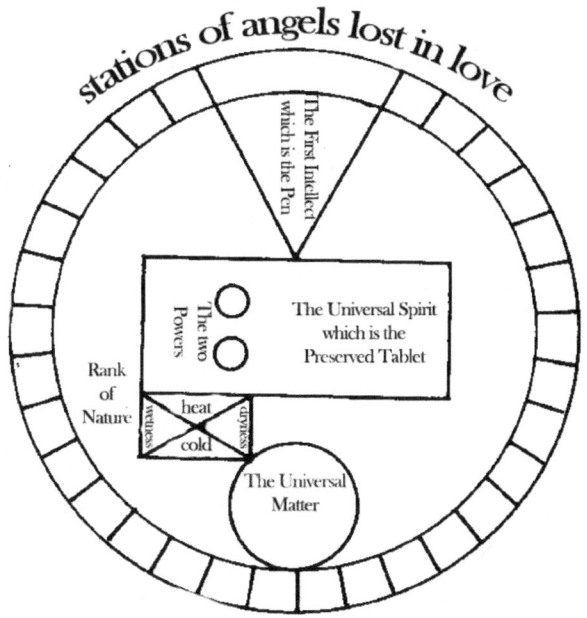

stations of angels lost in love

The First Intellect which is the Pen

The two Powers

The Universal Spirit which is the Preserved Tablet

Rank of Nature

wetness

heat

cold

dryness

The Universal Matter

"This is the image of the 'Primordial Cloud' and what it contains, culminating with the Divine Throne. Unfortunately, the image I have drawn here is too narrow to contain the forms of what we wish to include, in a single diagram. If I could draw a bigger diagram, it would have been clearer for the reader."

- *The Meccan Openings*, Vol VI, 186.

At the Summit of the Divine Throne

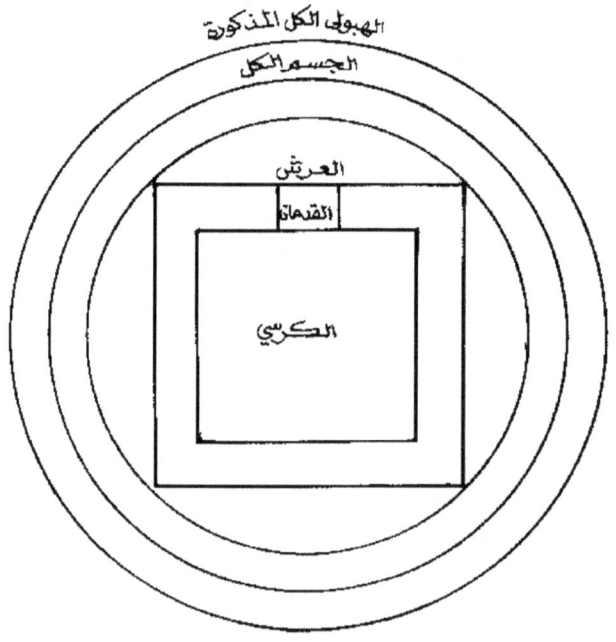

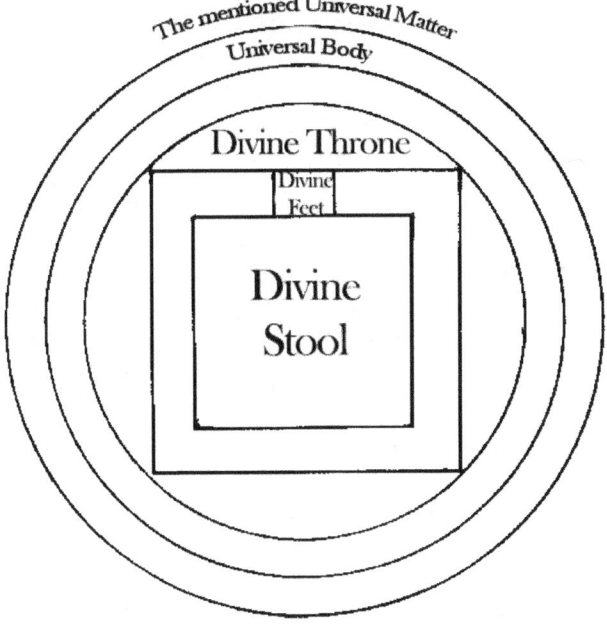

"This is the form of the Divine Throne, the Divine Stool, the water upon which the Throne resides and air which holds together this water and darkness."

- *The Meccan Openings*, Vol VI, 187.

The Horoscopes that Decorate Paradise

الكرسي المذكور

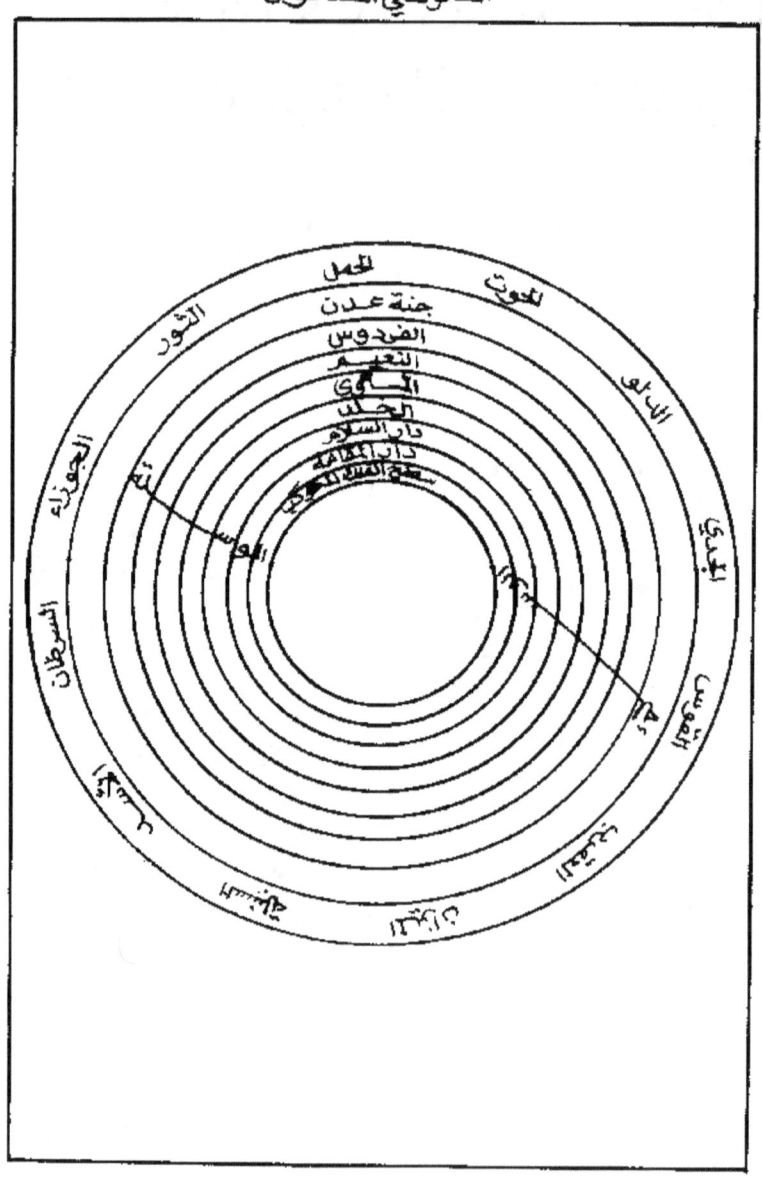

48

The mentioned Stool

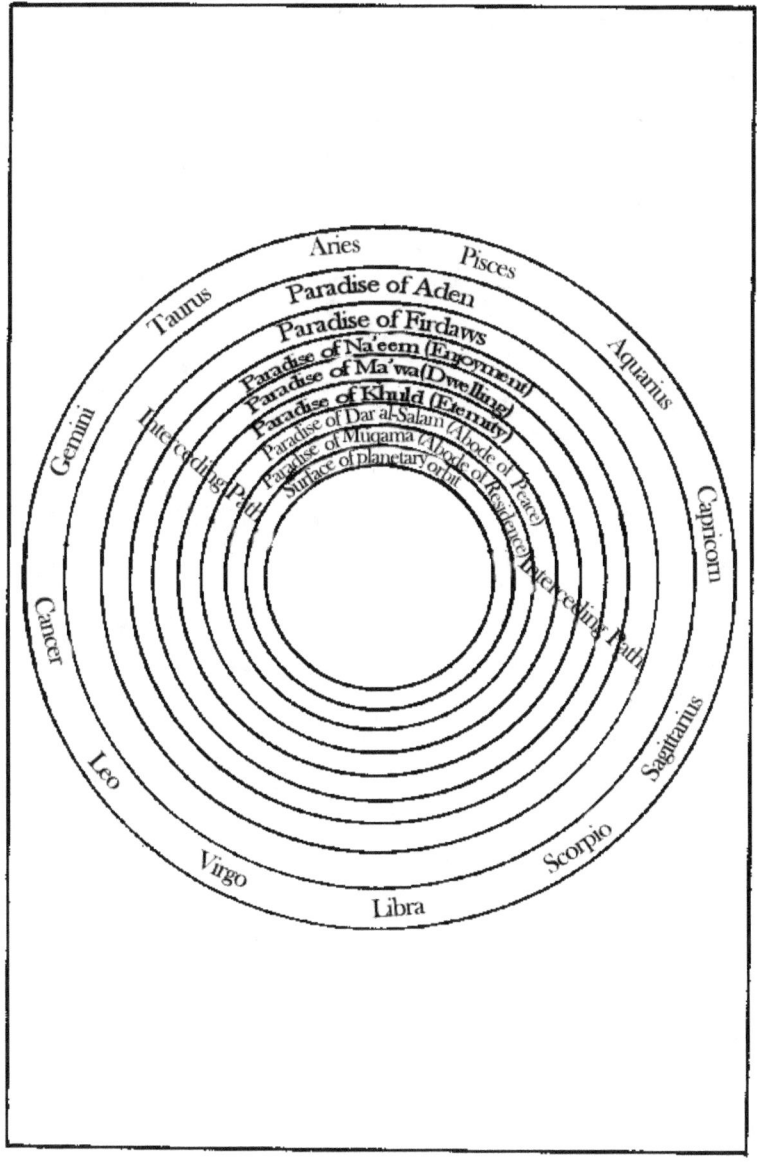

Aries
Pisces
Taurus
Aquarius
Gemini
Capricorn
Cancer
Sagittarius
Leo
Scorpio
Virgo
Libra

Paradise of Aden
Paradise of Firdaws
Paradise of Na'eem (Enjoyment)
Paradise of Ma'wa (Dwelling)
Paradise of Khuld (Eternity)
Paradise of Dar al-Salam (Abode of Peace)
Paradise of Muqama (Abode of Residence)
Surface of planetary orbit

Interceding Path

"This is a drawing of the outermost orbit, paradises, the surfaces of the planetary orbit and the tree of Touba."

-    *The Meccan Openings*, Vol VI, 188.

Cosmic Movement in the Starry Night Within

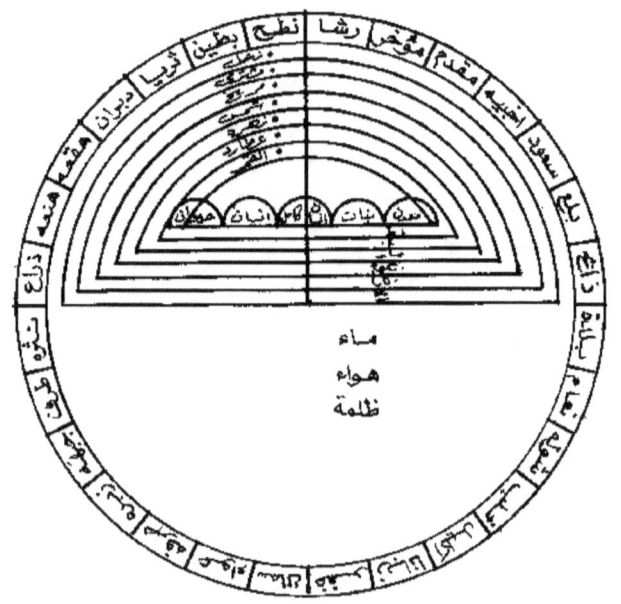

ماء
هواء
ظلمة

52

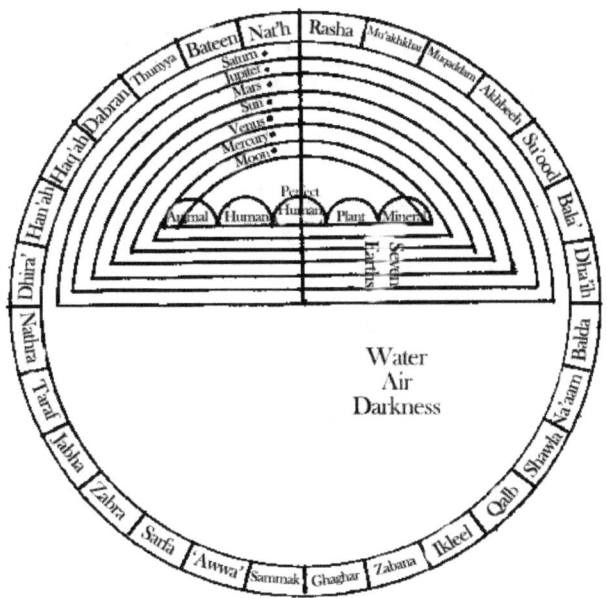

"This is the form of the planetary orbit, domes of the heavens and what they stabilize upon, namely the earth and three pillars through which God holds together the dome, minerals, plants, animals and human beings."

-   *The Meccan Openings*, Vol VI, 189.

A Palatial Organization for an August Occasion

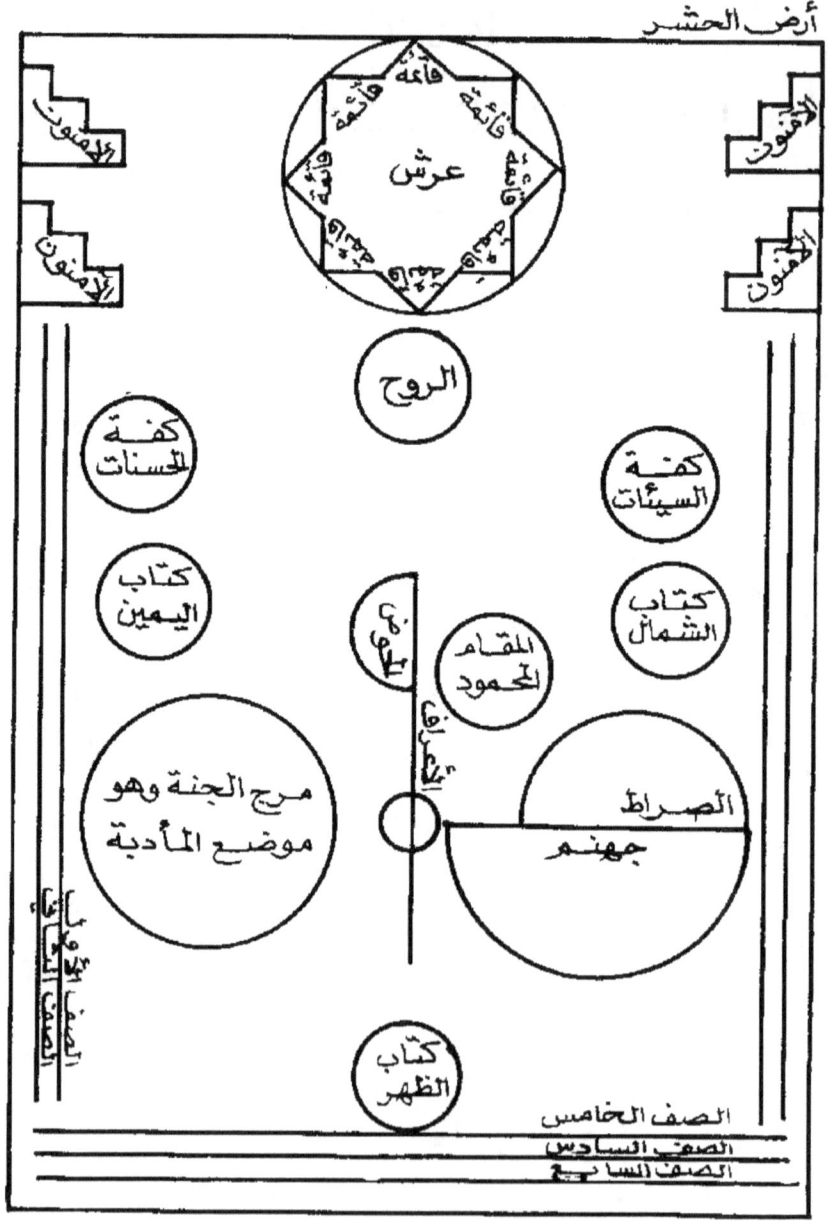

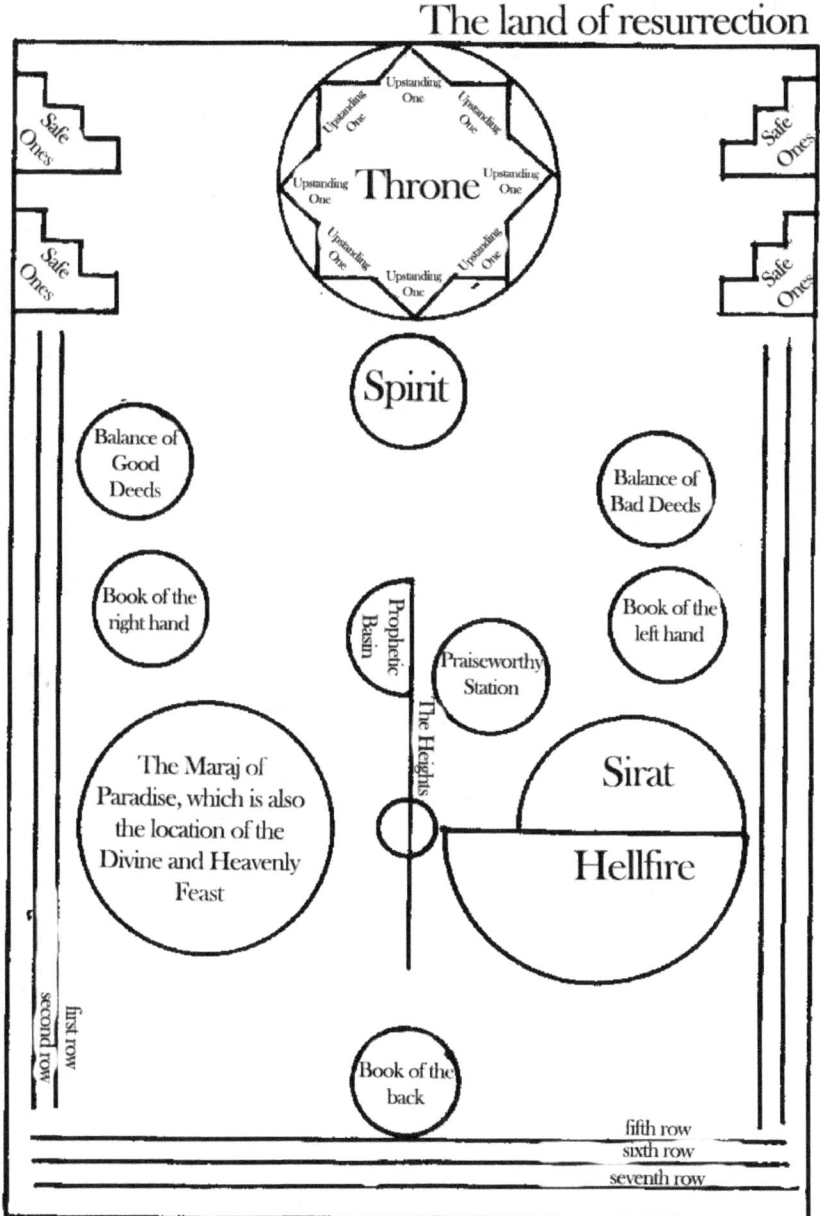

The land of resurrection

Throne

Upstanding One

Spirit

Safe Ones

Balance of Good Deeds

Balance of Bad Deeds

Book of the right hand

Prophetic Basin

Book of the left hand

Praiseworthy Station

The Heights

The Maraj of Paradise, which is also the location of the Divine and Heavenly Feast

Sirat

Hellfire

first row
second row

Book of the back

fifth row
sixth row
seventh row

"This is an image of the land of resurrection and what it contains of notable entities, ranks, the Throne of Delineation and Judgment, its carriers and the rows of angels."

- *The Meccan Openings*, Vol VI, 190.

Suffering at the Heart of Hearts and Veil

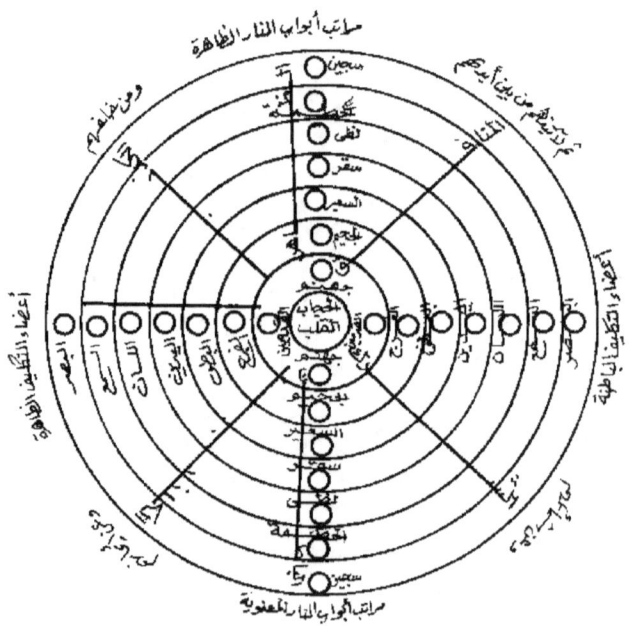

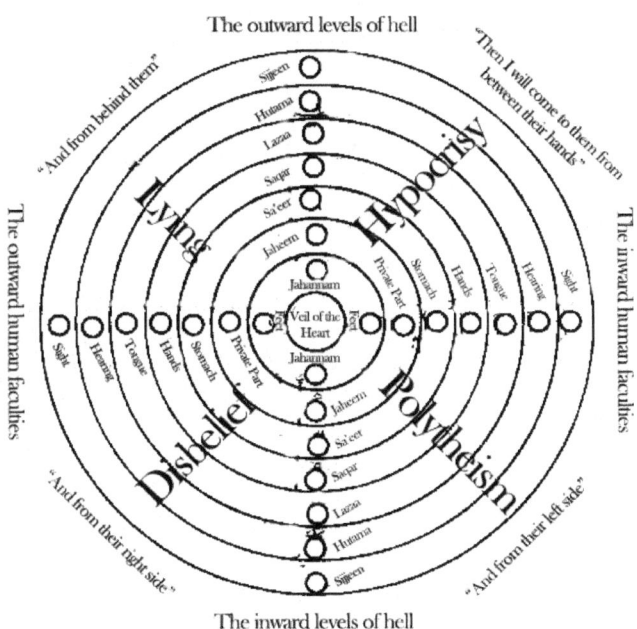

"This is an image of hellfire, its gates, levels and abodes."

- *The Meccan Openings*, Vol VI, 191.

The Conversation of Names that Began Everything

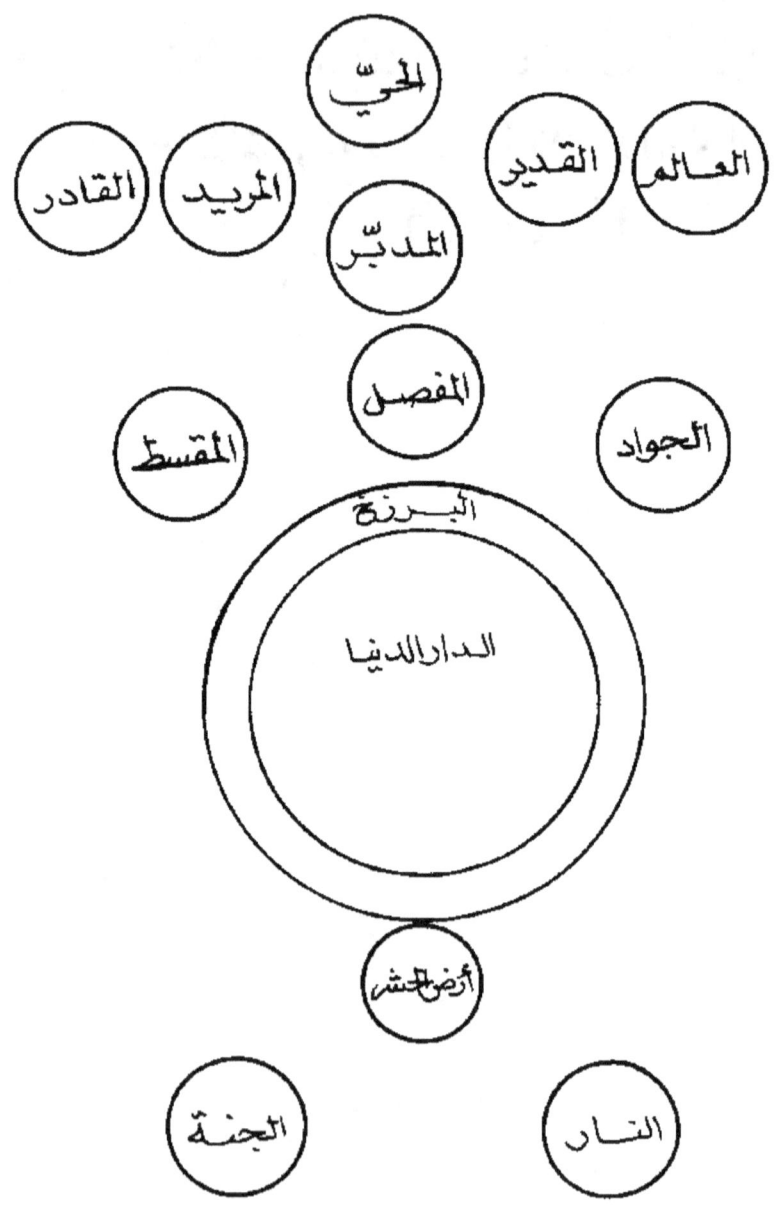

الحـي

العـالم القدير

القادر المريد

المدبّر

المفصـل

المقسط

الجواد

البـــرزخ

الـدار الدنيا

أرض الحشر

الجنـة

النــار

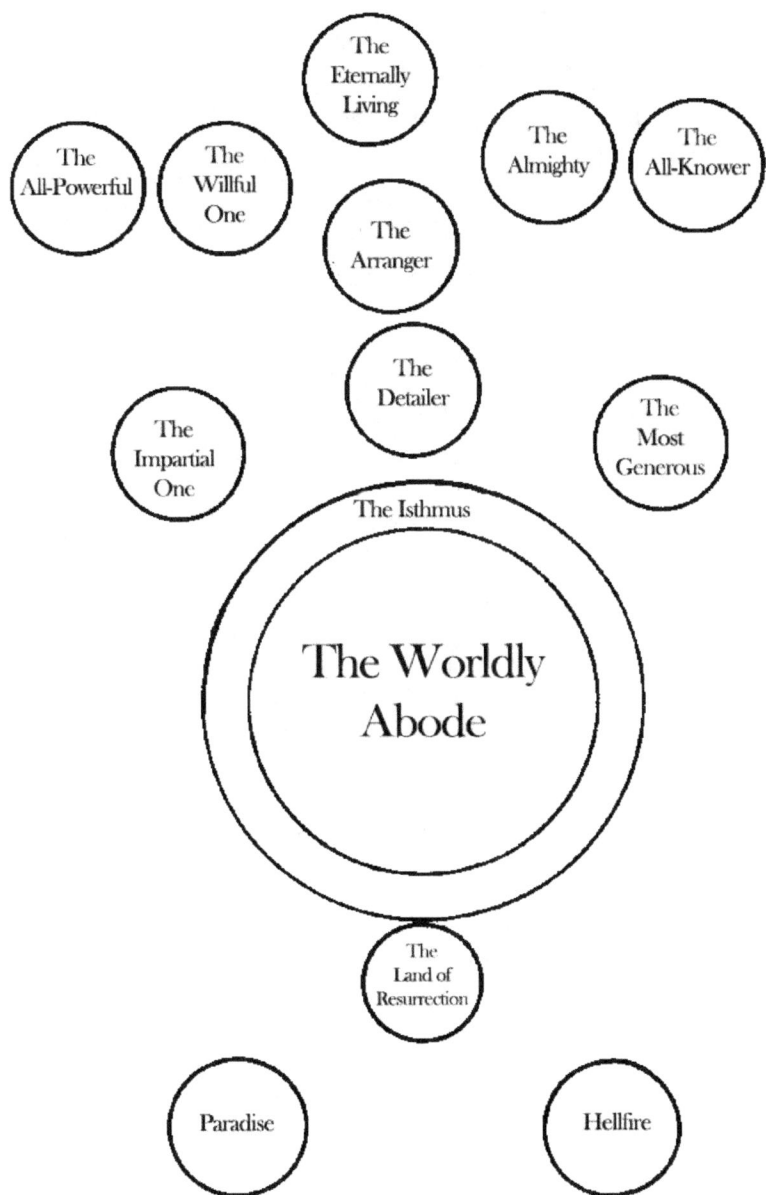

The Eternally Living

The All-Powerful

The Willful One

The Almighty

The All-Knower

The Arranger

The Detailer

The Impartial One

The Most Generous

The Isthmus

The Worldly Abode

The Land of Resurrection

Paradise

Hellfire

"This is an image of the Presence of Divine Names, this worldly life, the hereafter and *barzakh*."

- *The Meccan Openings*, Vol VI, 192.

A Beatific Vision Through Muhammadan Eyes

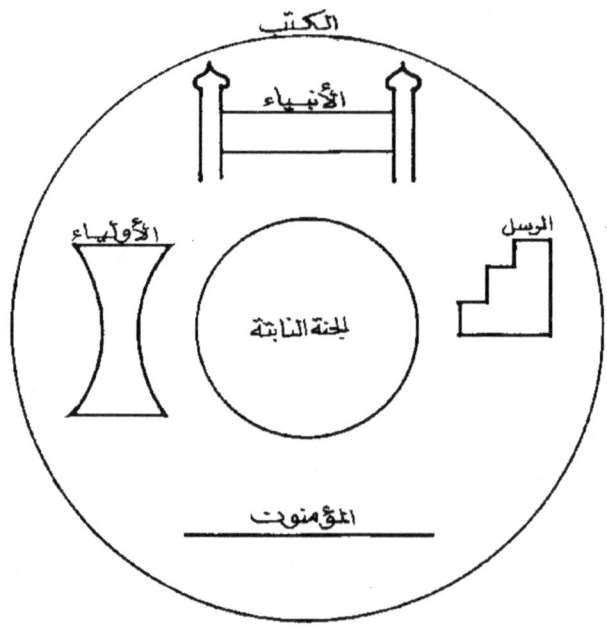

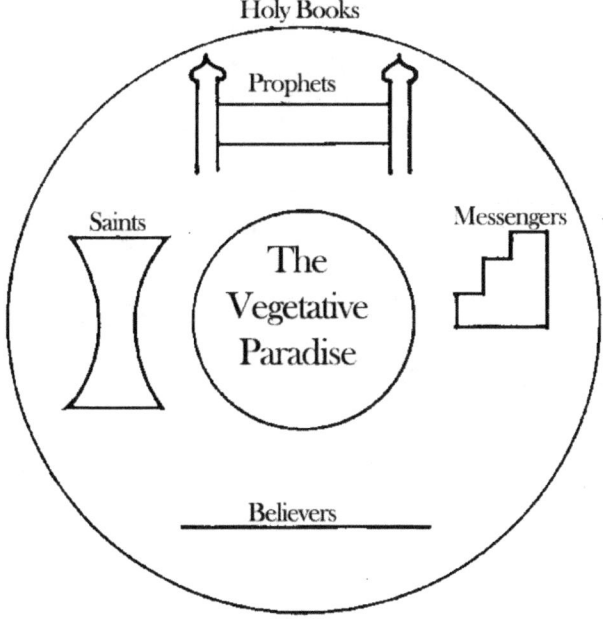

"This is an image of the *katheeb* (a land of musk in the paradise of Aden), wherein the beatific vision occurs and the different ranks of creation therein."

-   *The Meccan Openings*, Vol VI, 193.

The Simple Perfection
of a Heavenly Home

صورة الضراح

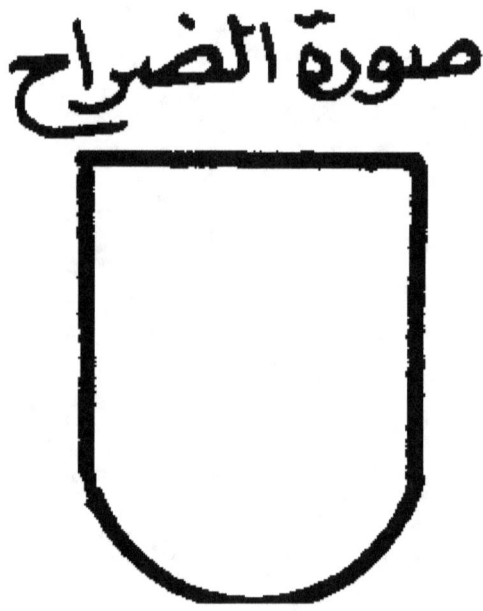

The Form of
Durah (Bayt al-Ma'mur)

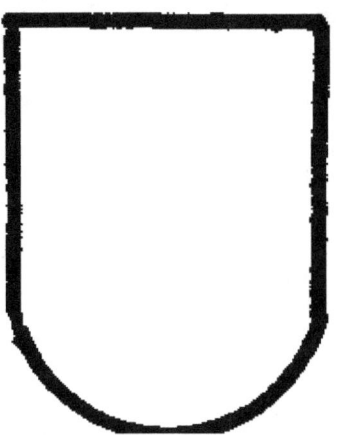

"On the surface of the seventh heaven resides the Durah, which is *al-Bayt al-Ma'mur* (the Established House). Its form is as I have drawn it here."

- *The Meccan Openings*, Vol VI, 207.

The Ecstatic Spiral of Love

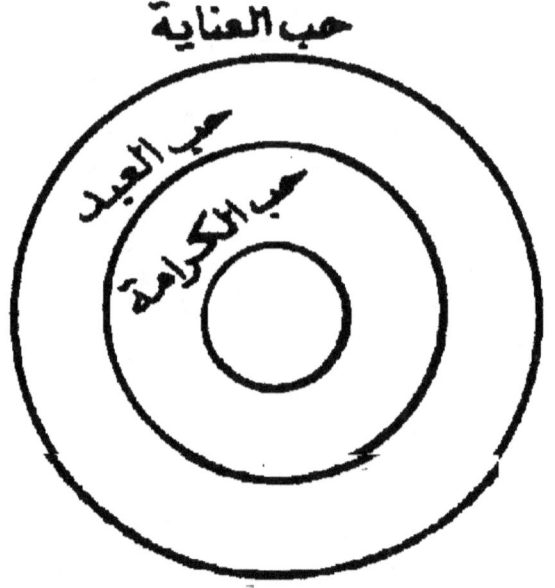

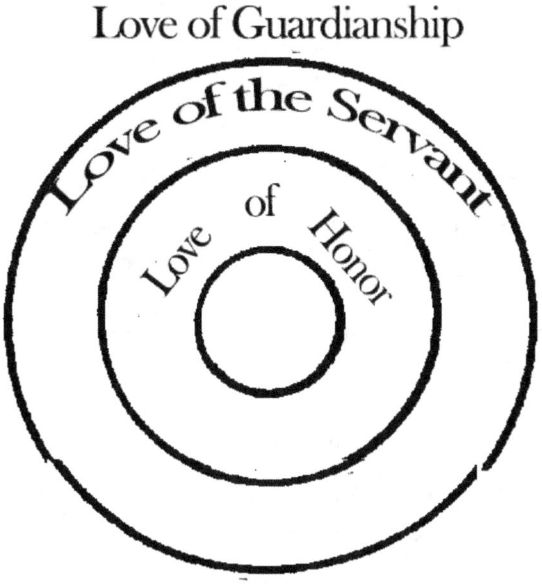

Love of Guardianship

Love of the Servant

Love of Honor

"God has informed us that He has servants whom He loves and who love Him. He made their love as an intermediary between two loves, from Him and to them.

He then granted them ease, through this love, to follow His Messenger (S) and obey what He brought of commands.

He then informed them that if they follow the Messenger, God will love them. This is a second love, unlike the first. For the first is a love of Divine Care, while the second is a love of reward and generosity.

The love of the servant remains between these two types of love. He is coerced in this intermediary love, in order to know that he is under the tight embrace of the Real. The affair is as we have drawn here."

- *The Meccan Openings*, Vol VI, 151.

Human Beings: A Spiritual Portrait

الحضرة القديمة

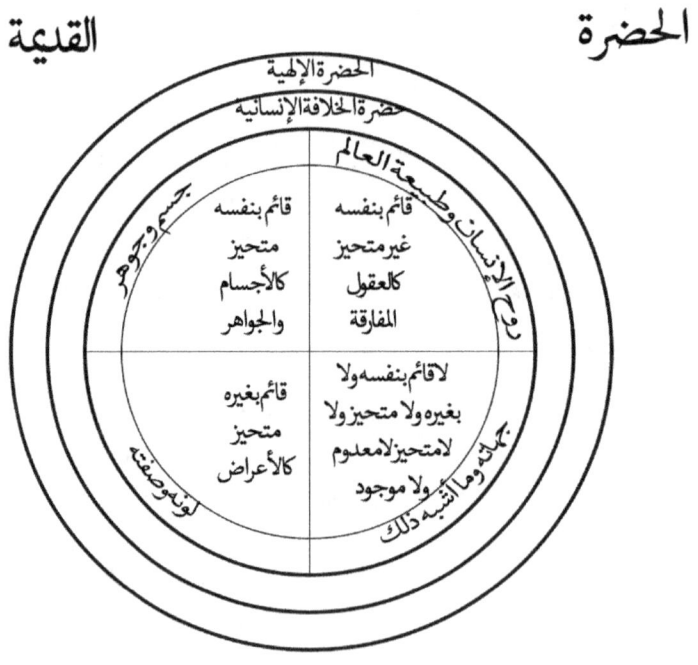

القديمة

الحضرة الإلهية
حضرة الخلافة الإنسانية
وطبيعة العالم

قائم بنفسه
غير متحيز
كالعقول
المفارقة

قائم بنفسه
متحيز
كالأجسام
والجواهر

لا قائم بنفسه ولا
بغيره ولا متحيز ولا
لا متحيز لا معلوم
ولا موجود

قائم بغيره
متحيز
كالأعراض

80

Ancient

Presence

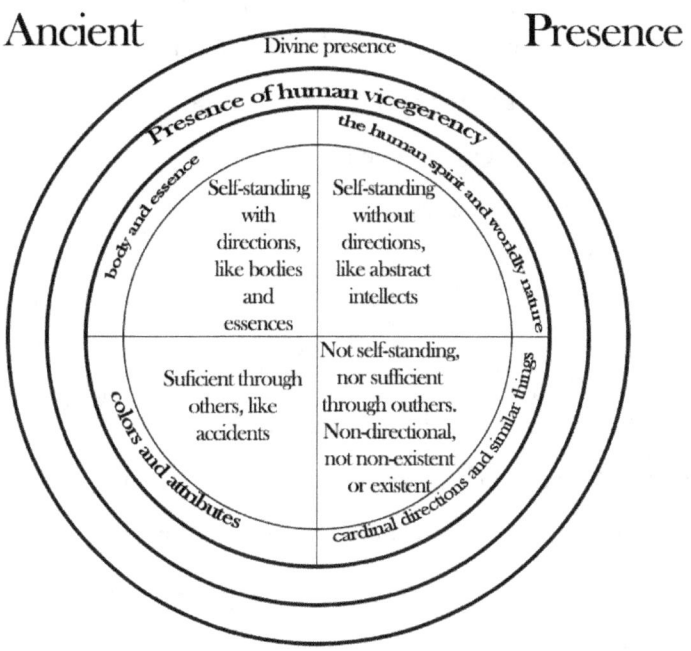

Divine presence

Presence of human vicegerency

the human spirit and worldly nature

body and essence

| Self-standing with directions, like bodies and essences | Self-standing without directions, like abstract intellects |
| Suficient through others, like accidents | Not self-standing, nor sufficient through outhers. Non-directional, not non-existent or existent |

colors and attributes

cardinal directions and similar things

"How honorable is this Reality and how pure is this Existent Being. But also, how lowly and filthy is it in this entire existence?

For from it emerged Muhammad (S), Abu Jahl, Moses and Pharaoh. So realize the perfected composition and place it in the center of those who are obedient and brought near. Also realize the lowest of the low and place it in the center of disbelievers and transgressors. And Exalted be He who has no likeness and He is the All-Hearing and All-Seeing!

The white circle, between the outermost black line is the example of the Divine Presence in Exaltedness. The adjacent white circle inside is that of the human being. In this way, the human being is between the Divine Presence and the universe."

-   *The Formation of Circles*, 150.

The Nine Hemispheres of the Essence

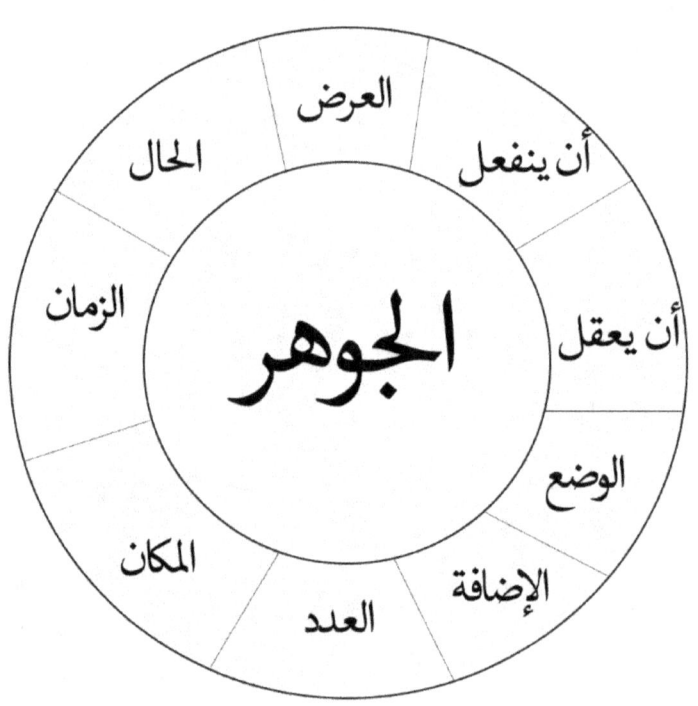

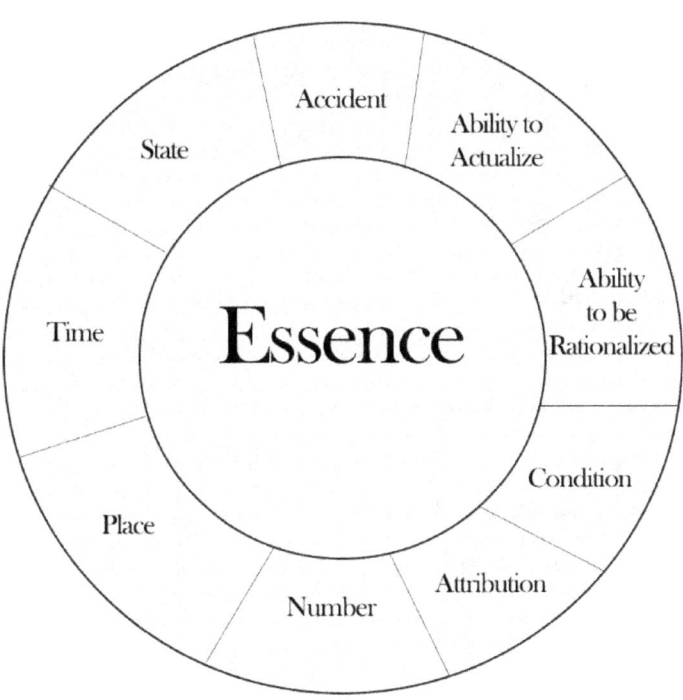

"The matrix of matter is the circle that encompasses all existent things absolutely. It contains all the known realities, whether existent, non-existent or non non-existent.

This is its form, if it were to have one. Since I have come to know it and actualize it, I have also been able to bring it out in a symbolic image, albeit in a condensed form.

The center of the circle is the dot of the Essence, which represents every self-standing essence, whether ancient or newly-created. Everything else, including colors, place, time and attributes appear as essences that are not self-sufficient."

- *Insha' al-Dawa'ir*, 151.

Bibliography

Ibn al-'Arabi, Muhammad. *Al-Futuhat al-Makkiyya*.
Beirut: Dar al-Kutub al-'Ilmiyya, 1994.
___, *Insha' al-Dawa'ir*. Beirut: Dar al-Kutub al-
'Ilmiyya, 1994.

The End

is just another beginning
in the circle of reality!

ومن الله التوفيق

الفاتحة

Ⳍⳋ